Nelson Spelling

Pupil Book 5

OXFORD
UNIVERSITY PRESS

Book 5 Scope and Sequence

Unit	Pupil Book Focus	Pupil Book Extra	Pupil Book Extension	Resource Book Focus	Resource Book Extension
1	**ar are** finding target words	identifying sound families	adding suffixes	letter patterns; word building	identifying root words
2	**word roots** arranging word families	word building	identifying Latin and Greek roots	sorting word families	identifying Latin and Greek word families
3	**ir ire** finding target words	identifying sound families	completing a wordsearch; writing definitions	letter patterns; identifying rhyming words	identifying word families
4	**y endings (nouns)** finding and using target words	target word quiz	using *ies* plurals	making *y* nouns	making *y* plurals; writing sentences
5	**adding s or es** identifying simple plurals	making *y* ending plurals	identifying singular/plural verb forms	making plurals; identifying pronouns	making plural nouns and singular verbs
6	**words ending a i o u** picture quiz	making *o* ending plurals	identifying word origins	picture matching	solving clues; completing a wordsearch
7	**silent letters** finding target words	identifying letter associations	alphabetical ordering	identifying silent letters; picture matching	writing sentences; correcting spellings
8	**unusual plurals** finding target words	making *f/fe* ending plurals	dictionary work; identifying irregular plurals	picture matching; writing plural nouns	working with tricky plurals
9	**able ible ably ibly** word building; word sums	identifying the *able/ible* rule	using *able/ible/ably/ibly* suffixes	letter patterns; word building; picture matching	using *able/ible/ably/ibly*; writing sentences
10	**mnemonics** identifying simple mnemonics	mnemonic quiz	identifying mnemonics; creating mnemonics	finding small words within words	creating mnemonics
11	**ow endings** letter patterns; target word quiz	sorting words by phoneme	working with syllables	using *llow/rrow*; completing a wordsearch	working with syllables
12	**et endings** writing missing vowel letters; target word quiz	recognising letter patterns	working with syllables	using *acket/icket/ocket*; completing crossword	working with syllables
13	**ull ul** finding target words	making adjectives	adding *ful* suffix; cloze activity	letter patterns; word building	solving clues; completing a wordsearch
14	**fer + suffixes** completing a wordsearch	doubling final *r*	alphabetical ordering	using suffixes	making word webs

The darker cells introduce statutory material for this year group in the National Curriculum for England.
The paler cells denote revision of a topic covered in previous years.

Unit	Pupil Book Focus	Pupil Book Extra	Pupil Book Extension	Resource Book Focus	Resource Book Extension
15	**hyphens and apostrophes** making contractions	making hyphenated prefixes	identifying hyphens and compound words	matching contractions; using hyphens	making contractions; writing sentences with compound /prefixed words
16	**ough** finding target words	identifying homophones	sorting by phoneme	using *ough/ought;* cloze activity; writing sentences	working with jumbled letters; writing definitions of homophones
17	**ost oll** finding target words and rhyming words	making *oll/oal/ole* words	adding *al/all*	using *ost/oll;* cloze activity; writing sentences	adding *l/ll;* writing sentences
18	**same letters, different sound** choosing rhyming words	sorting by phoneme	identifying *ear* pattern identifying; *ough* pattern	finding rhyming words using picture clues	sorting *ough* pattern; writing sentences
19	**homophones** finding target words; writing homophones	identifying near homophones	using homophones in sentences	writing and finding homophones	working with triple homophones
20	**ious eous cious tious** key word quiz	using *our/ous* rule; identifying root words	identifying *cious/tious* rule	letter patterns; finding *ous* words	checking spellings; writing sentences
21	**cal cial tial** completing a wordsearch	making adverbs; writing sentences	*identifying cial/tial* rule	word building; writing sentences	checking spellings; writing sentences
22	**ie** wordsearch; *ie* word quiz	using *f/fe* plurals	making word webs	word building; writing sentences	understanding the *ie* spelling rule
23	**ei** finding target words; completing a wordsearch	identifying *ie* rule	identifying *ei* homophones	word building	working with jumbled letters; cloze activity
24	**ey endings** letter patterns; target word quiz	making *y* ending plurals	identifying singular/plural verb forms	using *ey/ney/key;* completing a wordsearch	sorting *y* plurals
25	**ild, ind** cloze activity; letter patterns	identifying homonyms	adding prefixes and suffixes	word building; writing sentences	making word fans; cloze activity
26	**e or e** finding target words	word sums with *e + ing*	using e + vowel/consonant suffix	adding *ing;* cloze activity	building words with suffixes
27	**tricky words** completing a wordsearch	identifying double letters	frequent spelling problems	writing words from picture clues; cloze activity	using a dictionary to write definitions; correcting spellings
28	**using a thesaurus** finding synonyms	finding antonyms	writing sentences	verb/noun word quiz	finding synonyms; writing thesaurus entries

Be sm**ar**t. Cross with c**are**.
Stop for c**ar**s. Be aw**are**.

bark
barn

cart
smart
start
car

care
rare
fare
aware
beware
scare
spare
stare
share

Focus

A Look at these picture clues.
Write the **ar** and **are** words in your book.

1 _____ 2 _____ 3 _____

4 _____ 5 _____ 6 _____

B Copy these words neatly into your book.

ark   park   spark   sparkle   sparkler   sparklers

Write a sentence to describe what you notice about
their spellings.

A Sort the key words into sound pattern families and write them in your book, like this:

words with <u>ar</u> sounding like c<u>ar</u>	words with <u>are</u> sounding like c<u>are</u>
barn	fare

Add two more words of your own to each list.

B Write a sentence using one word from each family.

Make as many words as possible by adding a suffix, like this:

care + fully = carefully

Think **carefully!** Some words need to be adjusted slightly.

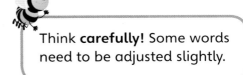

word box	suffix box
care	ly
art	ing
start	er
scare	fully
smart	ful
bark	ed

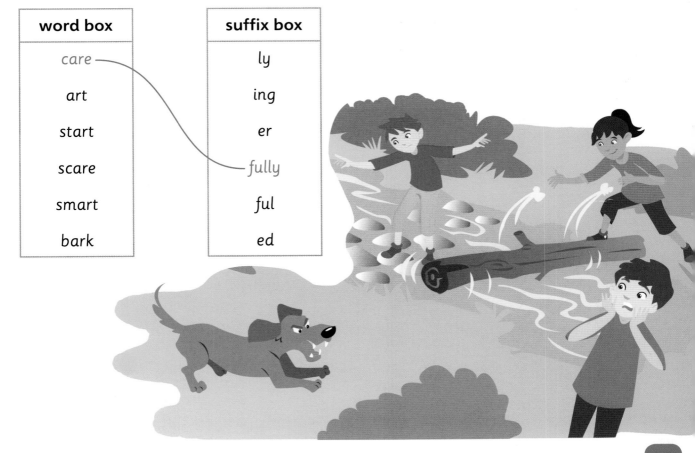

word roots

Focus

A Sort the words in the box into word families.
There are five families with three words in each family.

medic	relation	children	medicine	childhood
cover	childish	discovery	impressive	recover
expression	press	relate	medication	relatively

B Add at least one more word to each family.

Extra

Copy these words into your book. Make as many family words as you can. The prefixes and suffixes in the box might be helpful. The first one is done to help you.

un	in	re	im	en	over	de	dis
ing	ed	ly	ful	ment	en	ness	pre

1 joy   *enjoy joyful enjoying enjoyment enjoyable enjoyed*
2 take   **3** pain   **4** electric

Extension

Many words that we use in English today originally came from Greek or Latin. Here are some Greek and Latin words with their meanings:

Greek words

deka	ten
graphein	to write
hydor	water
metron	measure

Latin words

dicere	to say or tell
duo	two
frangere	to break
gradus	a step

A Copy the Greek and Latin words above into your book as a list. Next to each word write the two English words from the box that have been derived from these words.

gradual	dictate	fracture	speedometer	contradict	hydraulic
decimal	duet	duotone	fraction	decade	
grade	graphic	hydrant	autograph	thermometer	

B Write a simple definition of what each of these Greek and Latin words probably meant. Next to each write some English words that use these roots. The first one is done to help you.

	meaning	uses in English
magnus	*great or large*	*magnitude, magnify*
octo		
phone		
aqua		

Use a dictionary to help you.

7

The Firebird by Stravinsky

Third and final perfomance

For tickets enquire at the box office

Key Words

bird
third
shirt
skirt
first
thirsty

fire
wire
retire
inspire
expire
squire
enquire

Focus

Look at these picture clues.
Write the **ir** and **ire** key words in your book.

1 _____

2 _____

3 _____

4 _____

5 _____

6 _____

A Sort the key words into sound pattern families and write them in your book, like this:

words with <u>ir</u> sounding like f<u>ir</u>	words with <u>ire</u> sounding like f<u>ire</u>
bird	wire

Add two more words of your own to each list.

B Write a sentence using one word from each family.

a	c	q	u	i	r	e	s	u	j
g	d	e	s	i	r	e	q	h	j
b	m	n	g	t	r	x	u	n	g
t	h	q	i	n	s	p	i	r	e
f	n	u	b	w	r	i	r	a	h
s	h	i	r	e	e	r	e	x	g
f	c	r	n	v	d	e	q	b	g
c	p	e	r	s	p	i	r	e	d

A Make a list of the eight **ire** words hidden in the puzzle box.
Write a definition for each one in your book.
The first one is done for you.

squire   a country gentleman

B Sort the words in your list into alphabetical order.

Use a dictionary to help you.

9

y endings (nouns)

Cherry berry jelly –
Yucky mucky puppy!

Key Words

jelly
penny
berry
cherry
hobby
puppy

baby
lady
gravy
daisy
ivy
posy
story

Focus

A Look at these pictures.
Write the matching key words in your book.

1 _____

2 _____

3 _____

4 _____

5 _____

6 _____

B Write the key words that have double letters (like je**ll**y)
neatly in your book.
Next to each write a rhyming word.

C Write a sentence that has at least two key words.

A What am I?

1 I wag my tail when I'm pleased.   2 I grow on bushes.

3 I'm a small bunch of flowers.   4 I'm a tale in a book.

5 I'm a very young child.   6 I wobble a lot!

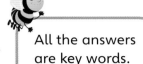

All the answers are key words.

B The words **dairy** and **diary** both end with **y**.
What else is interesting about them?
Use each in a sentence to show their meaning.

Extension

All these nouns end in **y**.

puppy   story   posy   baby   berry   lady

Remember, to make a noun that ends in **y** plural we usually change the **y** to **i** and add **es**, like this:

one pupp**y**   three pupp**ies**

But if the letter before the **y** is a single vowel letter, just add **s**.

pl**ay**   play**s**

A Finish these captions.

1 two _____

2 three _____

3 six _____

4 three _____

5 two _____

6 four _____

B Make a list of at least three other nouns that end in **y** where you need to change the **y** to **i** and add **es** to make the plural form.

C Make a list of at least three other nouns that end in **y** to which you just need to add **s** to make the plural form.

elephant**s**

boy**s**

pupp**ies**

fox**es**

Key Words

dog
dogs
elephant
elephants

dish
dishes
fox
foxes

baby
babies

boy
boys
trolley
trolleys

Focus

A Copy and finish the phrase to describe each of these pictures.
The first one is done to help you.

1 a pack of dogs   **2** a herd of _____   **3** twin _____

4 a stack of _____   **5** two _____   **6** a gang of _____

B Write a word that rhymes with each of these words and has the same spelling pattern.

1 boys   **2** dishes   **3** rays

As you know, when we make nouns **plural** we usually add **s** or **es**.
We add **es** if the word ends in **s, x, ch** or **sh**.

singular		plural
elephant + **s**	=	elephant**s**
dish + **es**	=	dish**es**

Remember, one thing is **singular**; more than one is **plural**.

A Write the plural form of these words. Can you spot the trick question?

1 school   2 bike   3 toothbrush   4 fox   5 pass
6 splash   7 watch   8 aeroplane   9 crash   10 mouse

Remember, to make a noun plural that ends with **y**, change the **y** to **i** and add **es**.

singular	plural
story	stor**ies**

But if the letter before the **y** is a single vowel letter (**a e i o u**), simply add **s**.

| toy | toy**s** |
| trolley | trolley**s** |

B Copy this table. Make the plural form of these nouns.

singular	monkey	cry	nappy	turkey	hobby	baby	chimney	jockey
plural								

Extension

Remember, strangely we often <u>add</u> **s** or **es** to make a verb singular!
But the same rules apply.

they run   he run**s**   they hurry   she hurr**ies**

Make these verbs singular. Use each one in a sentence.
The first one is done to help you.

1 terrify   *terrifies*   *The loud noise terrifies the kitten.*
2 hurry   3 jump   4 bury   5 defy

words ending with
a i o u

Can you see the kangaro**o** jumping past the big em**u**?

Focus

Look at these pictures and clues.
Write the key words in your book.

 1 a wild ox from North America

 2 a large spider with a deadly bite

 3 an Australian animal with a powerful kick

 4 an American wildcat

 5 an African antelope

 6 a wild dog from Australia

 7 a bird named after its call

There are special rules for making plurals for words that end with **o**. Usually we add **es**.

tomato   tomato**es**

But we simply add **s** for:

words ending in **oo**	cuckoo**s**
'music' words	piano**s**
shortened words	photo**s**

A Write the plural form of each of these nouns.

1 tornado   2 mango   3 cello   4 torpedo

5 domino   6 kangaroo   7 cuckoo   8 piano

B Using a dictionary, what can you discover about these words? Where did they come from? Are they a short version of a longer word?

1 photo   2 piano   3 disco   4 rhino   5 hippo

Extension

Most of the words that we use that end with a vowel letter other than **e** have come from a foreign language.

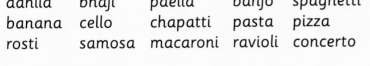

dahlia	bhaji	paella	banjo	spaghetti	emu
banana	cello	chapatti	pasta	pizza	risotto
rosti	samosa	macaroni	ravioli	concerto	

A Research the words in the box using dictionaries, reference books or searching online.

1 Sort them into lists according to the countries from which they came.

2 Make a list of the food words.

3 Make a list of the music words.

B The key words are all the names of creatures. Sort them according to the countries or regions they come from.

silent letters

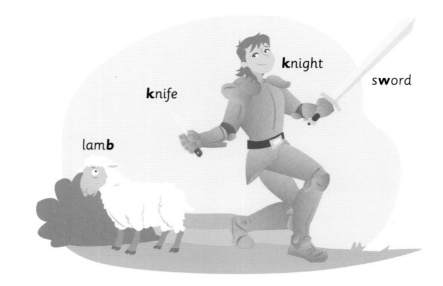

lam**b**   **k**nife   **k**night   **sw**ord

Key Words

lamb
thumb
doubt
subtle

solemn
autumn

thistle
whistle

knight
known
knuckle
knife

wreck
wrench
wrinkle
sword
answer

island
scissors
gnat
design

Focus

Look at these picture clues.
Write the key words in your book.

1 _____

2 _____

3 _____

4 _____

5 _____

6 _____

7 _____

8 _____

9 _____

Silent letters often have another particular letter next to them.

write   **wr**ong   **wr**inkle

A Write a sentence to say what you notice about the consonant letters next to the silent letters in each of these groups of words.

1 wrestle	wrapped	wreckage
2 gnome	gnaw	resign
3 lamb	numb	climber
4 scent	scenery	scissors
5 debt	doubt	subtle
6 knuckle	knock	knight
7 castle	bustle	listen

B Write as many words as you can to add to each of the word groups in **A**.

Write each of these groups of words in alphabetical order.

Check your answers in a dictionary.

1 lamb	thumb	combing	crumble
2 gnat	gnome	gnash	gnaw
3 knee	knelt	kneel	knew
4 write	wrong	wrapper	wrath
5 climb	comb	crumb	climbing

unusual plurals

The old **women** were tending the **oxen** and **geese** near the **chateaux**.

Focus

Read the key words and complete the phrase to describe each of these pictures.
The first one is done to help you.

1 a row of cliffs

2 three prickly _____

3 two _____

4 a herd of _____

5 two pairs of _____

6 two _____

To form the plural of nouns ending in **f** or **fe** we usually change the **f** or **fe** to **v** before adding **es**, like this:

shel**f** + s = shel**ves**   li**fe** + s = li**ves**

For nouns ending in **ff**, just add **s** to make the plural form.

pu**ff** + s = pu**ffs**

A Copy this table of singulars and plurals and fill in the blanks.

singular	half	calf	leaf	wife	life	sniff	self
plurals							

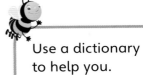

B Find the plural of **chief** and **belief**. What do you notice?

Use a dictionary to help you.

Most of the unusual plurals are related to nouns we have borrowed from other languages, such as Latin and French.

Here are a few examples:

aquar**ium**   aquar**ia**   curricul**um**   curricul**a**
chateau   chateau**x**   appendi**x**   append**ices**

Sometimes the words for the singular and plural are the same and for some singular nouns the plural is a different word altogether!

sheep   **sheep**   species   **species**
woman   **women**   person   **people**

Use a dictionary to find the unusual plurals for these words.

1 plateau   2 hippopotamus   3 man   4 cod
5 ox   6 appendix   7 index   8 analysis
9 phenomenon   10 goose   11 tweezers   12 child

able ible
ably ibly

There was a notice**able** change in the weather. The storm was incred**ible**!

Focus

A Choose a key word to complete these phrases.

1 a t_____ storm **2** my c_____ bed **3** the a____ kitten

4 the i__ dinosaur **5** the h_____ food! **6** the l____ puppy

B Copy and complete these word sums in your book. The first one is done to help you.

1 enjoy + able = *enjoyable*
2 reason + ably =
3 change + able =
4 ador + able =
5 horr + ible =
6 poss + ibly =
7 sens + ibly =

Remember, there is no easy way to know when to use **able** (or **ably**) and when to use **ible** (or **ibly**), but more words end in **able** than **ible**. Always check in a dictionary if you are not sure.

This tip will also help:
If a complete root word comes before the **able** or **ible** suffix, then it is probably an **able** word.

comfor**able**   understand**able**   reason**able**

Think carefully about the spelling tip and then choose an **able** or **ible** suffix for each of these words or letter groups.

1 depend   2 terr
3 agree   4 incred
5 invis   6 notice
7 respons   8 avail
9 enjoy   10 poss

Extension

The **able** suffix is used if another family word has the **ation** ending.

ador**ation**   ador**able**

Remember, when adding **able/ably** or **ible/ibly** to a word that ends with a single **e**, we nearly always first drop the **e**.

A Write the **able** word that is in the same word family as these words.

1 application   2 consideration   3 toleration   4 operation

B Do these word sums in your book.

1 invalue + able =   2 unbelieve + ably =
3 unrecognise + able =   4 sense + ibly =
5 incure + able =   6 irresponse + ibly =

mnemonics

My nan eats mountains of nachos in chilli sauce.

Key Words

teacher
library
reel
bicycle
necessary
separate
chocolate
lightning
twelfth
ambitious
vegetable
parallel
government
weight

Focus

A Write a short sentence explaining why each of these pictures can help you remember how to spell one of the key words.

1 vege<u>table</u>

2 <u>reel</u>

3 <u>teacher</u>

4 choco<u>late</u>

5 w<u>eight</u>

6 b<u>icy</u>cle

B Draw a small picture to remind you how to spell a word that you sometimes find difficult.

Mnemonics (pronounced 'nemonics') are short phrases
or rhymes that help us remember things. We can use
mnemonics to help us to be sure which homophone
to use.

here or **hear**   It's <u>here</u> not t<u>here</u>.
We h<u>ear</u> with our <u>ear</u>s.

A Copy these words and phrases. Underline the letters
that the mnemonic helps us to remember.

1 knight or night   The knight is the king's brother.
2 stake or steak   I leant the rake against the stake.
3 cellar or seller   The cellar is like a prison cell.
4 bear or bare   The bear bit my ear.

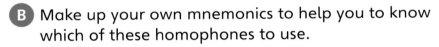

B Make up your own mnemonics to help you to know
which of these homophones to use.

1 groan or grown   2 fair or fare   3 check or cheque   4 pail or pale

Extension

A Copy the mnemonics below. In each one underline the
letters in each word that the mnemonic helps us to
remember. Use the mnemonics to learn how to spell the
six words.

1 separate   Rats never forget how to spell separate.
2 parallel   Parallel has two parallel lines in the middle.
3 device, advice, practice   Ice is a noun, as are device, advice, practice.
4 dictionary   Finn's dictionary won't help his diction.
5 government   Our government governs us.
6 necessary   Be careful of the cess pit in the middle
of necessary.

B Create mnemonics for these tricky words, or choose
some other words that you particularly want to learn.

1 lightning   2 chocolate   3 friend   4 innocent   5 island

ow endings

sparrow

burrow

hollow

shadow

Focus

A Copy these groups of words.
Underline the word in each group with the different letter pattern.

1 pillow   willow   shadow   billow

2 narrow   follow   sparrow   arrow

3 elbow   shallow   swallow   allow

B What am I?
Look at the picture clues and complete the sentences.
Then find the key word that matches the clue.
The first one is done to help you.

1 You rest your on me.   *pillow*

2 I am a small brown .

3 I'm home to a family of .

4 When the shines I never leave your side.

5 Mix me with and I turn green.

growl	known	prowl	show
growth	scowl	clown	slow
blown	brown	throw	crown
shown	down	frown	thrown

A Sort the words in the box into sound pattern families, like this:

words with <u>ow</u> sounding like c<u>ow</u>	words with <u>ow</u> sounding like wind<u>ow</u>
clown	slow

B Write a sentence using at least one word from each family.

Extension

Remember, a syllable is a part of a word that can be sounded by itself.
Each syllable has a vowel sound. For example:

pillow   **pil/low**   two syllables
arrow   **ar/row**   also two syllables

Notice how double letters are split between syllables.

grow	follow	following	rainbow
window	swallow	tomorrow	barrow
own	mower	borrowing	hollow

Sort the words in the box according to the number of syllables they have, like this:

one syllable	two syllables	three syllables
grow	follow = fol/low	following = fol/low/ing

et endings

A prize for every ball in the bucket!

Focus

A Each of these key words has had its vowel letters (**a e i o u**) taken out.
Write the complete words in your book.

1 j __ ck __ t

2 r __ ck __ t

3 t __ ck __ t

4 p __ ck __ t

5 w __ ck __ t

6 b __ ck __ t

B What am I?
1 I'm used in tennis and rhyme with packet.
2 I allow you to travel and rhyme with thicket.
3 I launch satellites and rhyme with socket.
4 I'm a game and rhyme with wicket.
5 I'm sewn on trousers and rhyme with locket.

Look carefully at these words.
Copy them into your book and underline the one that has
a different spelling pattern.

1 magnet	cabinet	tablet	bonnet
2 wicket	helmet	cricket	bucket
3 upset	droplet	triplet	pellet
4 socket	locket	ticket	gadget

Extension

> Remember, a syllable is a part of a word that can be
> sounded by itself.
> Each syllable has a vowel sound. For example:
>
> | | | |
> |---|---|---|
> | **let** | **let** | one syllable |
> | **blanket** | **blan/ket** | two syllables |

Copy these words. Put a line between the syllables.
The first one is done to help you.

1 gadget   *gad/get*

2 met

3 velvet

4 regret

5 regrettable

6 filleted

7 upsetting

8 bullet

9 puppet

10 trumpeting

11 pocket

12 rocket

ull ul

A b**ull** on a farm
Can do no harm.
A b**ull** in a china-shop
— Be caref**ul**!

Key Words

bull
bully
full
fully
pull
pully

dull
gull
gully

helpful
helpfully
painful
painfully

beautiful
beautifully

Focus

A Match a key word to each picture clue.

1 _____   2 _____   3 _____

4 _____   5 _____   6 _____

B Neatly copy five words that have the **fully** suffix into your book.
The key words will help you.

C Write a sentence using one of your **fully** words.

The suffix **ful** can be added to the end of some words to make an adjective, like this:

help   help**ful**   use   use**ful**

Notice that it only has one **l**.

Remember, an **adjective** is a **describing word**.

Add the **ful** suffix to make these words into adjectives.

1 shame   2 deceit   3 spite   4 pain   5 hope

6 wonder   7 thought   8 care   9 sorrow   10 doubt

Extension

If you are adding the suffix **ful** to a word ending with **y**, remember to change **y** to **i** before adding **ful**, like this:

plenty   plent**iful**

Exception: if the letter before the **y** is a vowel, we simply add **ful**, like this:

play   play**ful**

A Add the **ful** suffix to make these words into adjectives.

1 beauty   2 duty

3 fancy   4 mercy

B Use a word with the **ful** suffix to fill the gaps when you write these sentences.
The word in bold is a clue.

1 **beauty**   It was a _____ park.

2 **shame**   Everyone said it was _____ when it was dug up for a new road.

3 **dread**   They made a _____ mess and noise.

4 **hope**   We are _____ that the traffic won't cause too many accidents.

fer
+ suffixes

I pref**er** this refer**ee**.

refer
referring
referral
referred
reference
referee

prefer
preferred
preferring
preference

transfer
transferring
transferred
transference

Focus

A Copy the **fer** words in this puzzle box into your book. Can you find all eight words?

r	e	f	e	r	e	e	p	o	p	i	r
e	d	t	q	e	s	d	r	f	j	k	e
f	p	r	e	f	e	r	e	n	c	e	f
e	s	a	m	e	z	x	f	v	x	z	e
r	a	n	u	r	c	v	e	v	m	n	r
e	d	s	j	r	f	g	r	b	d	k	r
n	h	f	g	e	q	a	r	n	x	l	a
c	d	e	n	d	b	s	e	v	f	k	l
e	c	r	e	f	e	r	d	b	n	c	v

B Copy the words you have found that include **rr**.

Extra

When adding suffixes to words ending with **fer**, the **r** is doubled if the **fer** is stressed.

Listen to the sound the **fer** makes in each of these words.

re**ferr**ed   refe**r**ence

Make as many family words as you can for each of these root words by using the suffixes in the box.

ing   ed   ence   s   ee   al

1 refer
2 prefer
3 transfer
4 infer
5 defer
6 confer

Extension

A Write each of these lists of words in alphabetical order.

1 refer	referral	reference	referee
2 conference	conferring	confer	conferred
3 infers	inference	inferring	infer
4 prefer	prefers	preferential	preferring
5 transfer	transference	transferring	transferred
6 deference	deferred	deferring	defer

B Write a brief definition for each of these words.

1 referee
2 inference
3 deference
4 confer

Use a dictionary to help you.

Check-up 1

Focus

What are these? The first letters will give you a clue.
Write the words in your book.

1 c_____   2 sc_____   3 a_____   4 a_____

5 b_____   6 sp_____   7 p_____   8 b_____

9 b_____   10 f_____   11 k_____   12 l_____

13 s_____   14 m_____   15 t_____   16 sh_____

17 r_____   18 c_____able   19 b_____   20 r_____

Extension

A Write three words in the family of each of these words.

1 port   2 act   3 press

B Write the plural forms of these words.

1 baby   2 trolley   3 dish   4 play   5 potato
6 cello   7 woman   8 cactus   9 aquarium   10 deer

C Which letter often appears next to these letters when they are silent? For example **r** with **w** (**wr**ite).

1 g   2 b   3 k   4 t

D Make **able** or **ible** words from each of these.

1 enjoy   2 poss   3 incred   4 reason   5 sens

E Divide these words into syllables.

1 swallow   2 tomorrow   3 rainbow   4 upsetting   5 regrettable

F Add the **ful** suffix to make these words into adjectives.

1 shame   2 care   3 hope   4 plenty   5 beauty

G Add the **ed** suffix to these words.

1 transfer   2 infer   3 refer   4 prefer   5 defer

hyphens and apostrophes

Please **co-operate**.
Don't *try to* **re-enter**
after the **re-start**.

Focus

Apostrophes are used to show where a letter or letters have been omitted when two words are run together and shortened. These are called **contractions**.

| he will | **he'll** | was not | **wasn't** |

A Write the contractions for these words in your book. The first one has been done to help you.

1 she will = *she'll*

| 2 I am | 3 have not | 4 must not | 5 could not |
| 6 do not | 7 she is | 8 cannot | 9 were not |

B Write these contractions in full. The first one has been done to help you.

1 they'll = *they will*

2 he's	3 they're
4 there's	5 won't
6 can't	7 we're
8 let's	9 they'll

Hyphens are sometimes used to join a prefix to a root word, especially if the prefix ends in a vowel and the root word also begins with one.

co-operate   **re-a**pply

A Choose a key word to match each of these definitions.

1 to work together positively
2 to be the joint owner of something
3 not prepared to give a firm answer
   to a question
4 the coated surface on a cooking pan
5 to apply again for something
6 to enter again
7 popular and widely recognised
8 to help to arrange or organise

B Use a dictionary to help you find and list some other words that include hyphens. Start by looking at **co-**, **non-** and **re-** words.

Extension

Hyphens are also sometimes used to make compound words. Most of these are adjectives, like this:

sugar-free   **well-known**   **open-mouthed**

accident-prone	computer-aided	good-looking
sugar-free	power-driven	quick-thinking
carbon-neutral	over-rated	bad-tempered
sport-mad	custom-built	fair-haired
oven-ready	well-known	open-mouthed

Use five of the hyphenated words in the box in sentences of your own.

The sea can be angry
*The sea can be r**ough***
The sea can be vicious
*The sea can be t**ough**.*

John Foster

Key Words

rough
enough

cough
trough

dough
though

nought
bought
brought
thought

bough
plough

Focus

Match a key word to each picture.
Write them in your book.

1 _____

2 _____

3 _____

5-5=

4 _____

5 _____

6 _____

7 _____

8 _____

9 _____

Extra

These sets of words have very similar sounds so they can cause some spelling problems.

A Copy these sentences neatly into your book, selecting the correct words.

Remember, words like these are called **homophones**.

It was a **rough/ruff** morning. **Boughs/Bows** were falling from the trees, but the baker **fort/fought** his way to the village bakery.
He knew his hot crusty bread was much **sought/sort** after by the tourists and no sooner had he started baking his first batch of **doe/dough** than he saw his first customers of the day peeping in **threw/through** his window.

B Use a dictionary to check your answers.

Extension

Read the key words.

A 1 Write the words where the **ough** sounds like **off**.

  2 Write the words where the **ough** sounds like **uff** in **fluff**.

  3 Write the words where the **ough** sounds like **ow** in **how**.

  4 Write the words where the **ough** sounds like **ow** in **snow**.

B

| laughter | taught | caught | laugh | daughter |
| slaughter | laughing | naughty | draughts |

Beware! The letter pattern **augh** can sometimes make a similar sound to **ough** in **bought**, or sometimes it sounds like **ar** in **park**.

Sort these nine words into two sets according to the sound made by the **augh** letter pattern.
Write a fun sentence using as many of the **augh** words as you can.

ost
oll

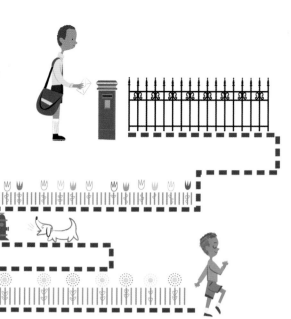

You alm**ost** missed the
p**ost** because you just
str**oll**ed down the road!

Key Words

post
host
most
almost

roll
toll
stroll
scroll
swollen

Focus

A Look at these picture clues.
Write the **ost** or **oll** words in your book.

1 _____

2 _____

3 _____

4 _____

5 _____

6 _____

B 1 Write two words that rhyme with **cost**. The first letters
will give you a clue.

l_____   fr_____

2 Write three words that rhyme with **most**.

3 Write four words that rhyme with **stroll**.

The letter patterns **oll**, **oal** and **ole** usually make the same sound.
Look at the clues and the first letters of these words.
Each word needs one of the letter patterns. Write the answers in your book.

1 f_____ a young horse
2 r_____ small type of bread
3 h_____ space left when something is removed
4 c_____ black lumps of rock that burn
5 st_____ a gentle walk
6 st_____ what the thief did
7 p_____ often has a flag on top
8 sh_____ large group of fish

Extension

Say these words quietly to yourself:

also   almost   ball   tall

Notice that when the **al** pattern comes at the beginning of a word it is usually spelt with one **l**, but when it comes at the end of a word it is often spelt with two.

Remember, **all right** is always <u>two</u> words!

A Add **all** or **al** to make these words. If you are unsure of any, check them in a dictionary.

1 ____so   2 ____ready   3 sm____   4 ____though

5 ____together 6 ____ways   7 st____   8 ____mighty

B Put the words that you have made in alphabetical order.
Remember to look at the third, or the fourth, letter.

same letters, different sounds

What on **ear**th shall
we w**ear**?
I f**ear** we'll never decide!

Focus

A Write the rhyming words in your book.
The picture clues will help you.

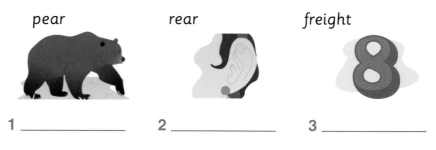

pear   rear   freight

1 _____   2 _____   3 _____

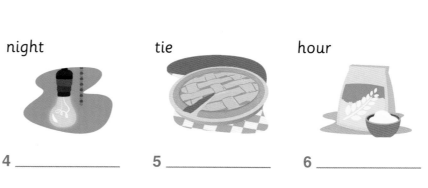

night   tie   hour

4 _____   5 _____   6 _____

B Add another word that rhymes and has the same
spelling pattern as each of the words that you
have written.

Some letter patterns have more than one sound.
For example:
   the gr**ea**t b**ea**st's h**ea**d

1 Sort the words in the box into lists according to the sound the **ea** pattern makes. Some words go into more than one list.

weather	jealously	read	heater	break	treasure
measuring	streak	meat	seating	reader	bread
steak	greater	lead	beating	greatly	heavenly

ea sounds like **e** in h**e**n	**ea** sounds like **ai** in p**ai**n	**ea** sounds like **ee** in f**ee**t
weather	break	streak

Words that can go into more than one box are **homophones**.

2 Which of the words in the box went into more than one list?

Extension

A Sort the words in Box A into lists according to the sound the **ear** pattern makes.

Box A

| rear | earn | year | dear | learn | yearn |
| beard | search | near | heard | gear | earth |

B Sort the words in Box B into lists according to the sound the **ough** pattern makes.

Box B

| bough | thought | plough | wrought | bought |
| enough | though | brought | drought | sought |

Beware! In **Box B** two of the words are in lists by themselves.

homophones

The **draught** blew the first **draft** of my story out of the window.

Focus

A Look at these picture clues.
Write the correct word in your book.

1 _____   2 _____

3 _____   4 _____

B Write a homophone for each of these words.

1 bridal

2 aloud

3 draft

Remember, **homophones** are words that sound the same but are spelt differently and have different meanings.

Sometimes words are not actually homophones, but they still sound very similar.

We can't **accept** foreign coins, **except** for charity.

Remember, **homo** means same and **phone** means sound.

A Write these words in your book.
Next to each one write a homophone, or near homophone, from the box.

wary	whose	effect	proceed	principal
past	morning	led	herd	guessed

1 who's   2 weary   3 affect   4 precede

5 principle   6 passed   7 mourning

8 lead   9 heard   10 guest

B Use a dictionary to help you write definitions for two of the pairs of homophones in **A**.

Extension

Use each of these near homophones in a sentence that shows its meaning.

1 eligible   illegible

2 dissent   descent

3 desert   dessert

4 eliminate   illuminate

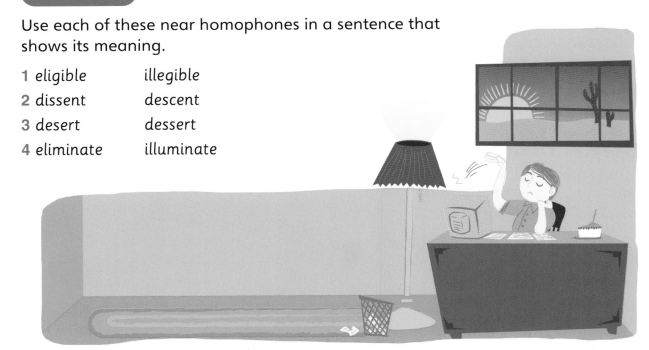

ious
eous
cious
tious

curious

Key Words

anxious
curious
furious
previous
victorious

hideous
courteous

vicious
precious
conscious
delicious
malicious
suspicious

ambitious
cautious
fictitious
infectious
nutritious

Focus

Match a key word to each of these definitions.

1 food that is likely to be good for you

2 something loved and valued

3 looks horrible

4 wildly aggressive

5 wanting to find out

6 very cross

7 careful

8 someone with a disease that might be passed on

9 keen to do well

10 tasty

Remember, when adding the suffix **ous** or **ious** to words ending with **our**, first drop the **u** in the word to which the suffix is added, like this:

vapour   vapor**ous**

A Copy these words into your book and then, next to each one, write the word with the **ous** or **ious** suffix added.

The last one is tricky!

   1 victor   **2** labour   **3** vigour   **4** glamour

There are other tricky letters in some **ous** words.
If there is an 'i' (as in h<u>i</u>t) sound, it is usually spelt as 'i', like this:

ser**i**ous   fur**i**ous

B Copy each of these words in your book and next to each one write its 'root' word.
The first one is done to help you. What do you notice?

   1 furious *fury* **2** various **3** glorious **4** victorious **5** anxious

C Copy each of these words in your book and next to each one write its 'root'. What do you notice?

   1 hideous   **2** gorgeous   **3** outrageous   **4** courageous

Extension

Tip 1: When adding the **ious** suffix, if the root word ends in **ce** there is usually a **c** before the **ious**, like this:

gra<u>ce</u>   gra<u>c</u>ious

Tip 2: If there is a family word that ends **tion** then there is usually a **t** before the **ious**, like this:

ambi<u>tion</u>   ambi<u>t</u>ious

You might need to check the last one in a dictionary!

Write the **ious** family word for these words. Consider the tips in the box carefully.

1 space   **2** vice   **3** infection   **4** malice

5 caution   **6** nutrition   **7** ambition   **8** fiction

cal cial tial

musical

Focus

A Copy the **al** words in this puzzle box into your book. Can you find all ten words?

c	o	n	f	i	d	e	n	t	i	a	l
l	i	n	i	t	i	a	l	r	c	b	o
i	p	a	r	t	i	a	l	o	r	j	f
n	d	e	z	c	g	h	q	p	u	z	f
i	b	g	s	s	p	e	c	i	a	l	i
c	o	m	i	c	a	l	g	c	k	q	c
a	e	s	s	e	n	t	i	a	l	r	i
l	c	m	u	s	i	c	a	l	d	d	a
c	o	m	m	e	r	c	i	a	l	v	l

B Copy the words you have found that end with **cial** or **tial**.

To make an adverb from an adjective we usually add the suffix **ly**.

quick   quick**ly**   comical   comical**ly**

Notice that if the adjective ends in **l** we still add **ly**. Don't be tempted to drop one **l**, you need them both!

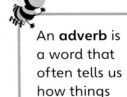

An **adverb** is a word that often tells us how things are done.

A Copy these words into your book then, next to each one, write the adverb.

1 musical   2 clinical   3 mechanical   4 special   5 official

6 essential   7 confidential   8 financial   9 artificial   10 partial

B Write three sentences. Each sentence must include at least one of the words you have just made.

Extension

When wondering whether to spell a word with **cial** or **tial** at the end, remember that **cial** usually comes after a vowel letter whereas **tial** comes after a consonant, like this:

off**i**cial   pa**r**tial

vowel letter   consonant letter

A Finish these words, adding either **cial** or **tial**.

1 offi_____   2 par_____   3 spe_____   4 confiden_____

5 essen_____   6 spa_____   7 artifi_____ 8 ini_____

B These words don't follow the rule. Write them in your book. Next to each write its root word.
Can you suggest why they end in **cial** even though a consonant letter comes before the suffix?

1 commercial   2 financial   3 provincial

ie

Good grief! Would you believe it?

brief
grief
chief
thief
frieze
field
shield

belief
believe
relief
relieve

Focus

A Find the **ie** key words hidden in the puzzle box. Write the words in your book.

b	i	k	j	g	e	f	s
h	f	b	x	r	d	r	h
g	r	e	r	i	c	i	i
b	e	l	i	e	v	e	e
r	l	i	v	f	l	z	l
i	i	e	s	a	m	e	d
e	e	f	t	h	i	e	f
f	f	i	e	l	d	n	o

B Write the answers to this quiz in your book. All the answers are **ie** words.

1 What is a name for someone who steals?

2 What do sheep graze in?

3 What is great sadness?

4 What does a knight carry for protection?

To make plurals from nouns that end in **f** or **fe** we usually change the **f** to **v** and add **es**, like this:

one thief, two thie**ves**   one life, two li**ves**

Sometimes, but not often, we simply add **s**, like this:

one chief, two chief**s**

Copy these words. Next to each one write its plural form and a sentence with the word in it. The first one has been done to help you.

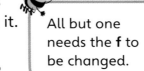

All but one needs the **f** to be changed.

1 thief   thieves   The thieves stole my bike.

2 loaf   **3** wolf   **4** shelf   **5** leaf

6 chief   **7** life   **8** knife   **9** wife

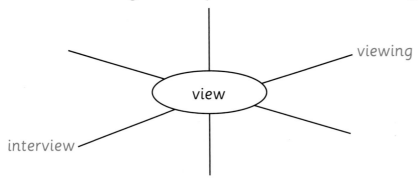

A **View** is the root for many other words. Draw a word web and add as many words containing **view** as you can. Here are some to get you started.

```
                              viewing

            view

interview
```

Don't forget that you can add prefixes (like **inter** and **re**) and suffixes (like **er**, **ed** and **ing**) or both, to build the words.

B Can you think of another word to use as the centre of a word web? Make a word web of your own.

ei

Gran is **ei**ghty-**ei**ght today!

Focus

A Which key words match the pictures?

1 _____   2 _____   3 _____

B Write the key words that you can find hidden in this puzzle box.
Some words can be found more than once!

v	t	r	s	i	e	r	e	y
f	g	f	l	e	i	s	i	v
i	s	h	e	i	g	h	t	e
e	r	e	i	n	h	r	w	i
m	e	i	g	h	t	e	e	n
e	i	g	h	e	y	i	i	y
g	g	h	a	r	x	n	g	o
h	n	t	s	y	a	s	h	n
f	f	r	e	i	g	h	t	l

This rule will help you to remember whether the **i** comes before or after the **e**.

i comes before **e**	pi**e**ce, reli**e**f
except after **c**	re<u>c</u>**e**ive, <u>c</u>**e**iling
or when the sound is not **ee**	for**fei**t, r**ei**gn

1 Copy these words into your book.

> receive   their   sleight   field   deceit   leisure   believe
> rein   achieve   wield   chief   shield   vein   eight   receipt

2 Tick the words in which the **ie** or the **ei** sounds **ee**.

3 Underline the ones that you have ticked that have an **ei**.

4 What do you notice about the words that you have underlined?

5 What do you notice about the words that you have not underlined or ticked?

Look at the homophones in the box.
Choose three sets and use your dictionary to find out what each word means.
Write or illustrate the definitions in your book. The first one has been done to help you.

> **Homophones**
> sound the same but have different spellings and meanings.

reign	weigh	eight	weight	sleigh	vein	ate
rein	way	wait	slay	vane	rain	vain

rein   reign   rain

ey endings

Look at that monkey on the chimney!

Key Words

abbey
alley
valley
donkey
monkey
honey
money
jockey
trolley
chimney
chutney
turkey
journey

Focus

A Copy these groups of words.
Underline the word in each group with the different letter pattern.

1 monkey	chutney	donkey	turkey
2 jockey	money	chimney	honey
3 alley	abbey	valley	trolley

B What am I?
Look at the picture clues and complete the sentences. Then find the key word that matches the clue. The first one has been done to help you.

1 I race  .   *jockey*

2 I am very good at climbing .

3 I am on top of a .

3 I am on top of a .

4 I'm made by .

Remember, when we add **s** to most words ending in **y** we change the **y** to **i** and add **es**, like this:

one loll**y**   three loll**ies**

But if the word ends in a single **vowel (a e i o u) + y**, we simply add **s**, like this:

one monk**ey**   three monkey**s**

Make these nouns plural.

1 toy	2 trolley	3 lady	4 fly
5 chimney	6 jockey	7 runaway	8 guy
9 difficulty	10 valley	11 activity	12 injury
13 boy	14 donkey	15 battery	16 monkey

Remember, a **noun** is a **naming word**.

Extension

Look again at the rules in the Extra section.
When we need to add **s** to a verb, the same rules apply.

Copy these sentences and write a verb ending in **s** to fill each gap. The words in brackets will help you.

Dad always (fly) into a rage when Spot (bury) his bone in the vegetable patch.

"That new puppy always (defy) me!" shouted Dad angrily.

"I think he (try) to make me mad! Who (pay) for all the new plants – him or me?"

ild
ind

In the labyrinth, paths twist and w**ind**.
Answer the riddles. What will you **find**?

Key Words

mild
wild
child

bind
find
kind
mind
wind
blind
grind

Focus

A Look at the picture of the labyrinth.
Copy these sentences and fill the gaps with key words.

"I can't f_____ my way," said the woman.

"Would you m_____ helping me?" she asked.

"No, I don't m_____," said the c_____ .

"You are very k_____," replied the woman with a smile.

B Copy these groups of words. Underline the word in each
group that has a different letter pattern.

1 mild   wild   find   child   children
2 kind   grind   pint   find   wind
3 grind   ground   mind   bind   minder

Remember, words that are spelt the same and sound the same but have different meanings are called **homonyms**.

Look at the two pictures below.

She was very **kind** to her brother.

What **kind** of dog do you like best?

Write two sentences for each of these homonyms to show that they can have two different meanings.

1 bank   2 bow   3 bark   4 bat   5 watch

Extension

We sometimes add prefixes to the beginning of words and suffixes to the end of words, like this:

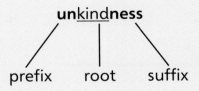

un<u>kind</u>**ness**

prefix   root   suffix

Copy these words into your book. Underline the root word of each.

1 remind   2 unwinding   3 rewinding   4 unkindly

5 children   6 minder   7 grinding   8 wilderness

9 blindingly 10 reminds   11 childish   12 kindness

e or e̶?

shak**e**   shaking   smil**e**   smiling

Key Words

shake
shaker
shaking

cure
curing
curable

close
closing
closed

ride
riding

smile
smiling

Focus

A Match a key word ending in **ing** to each of these actions.

1 c_____   2 r_____

3 s_____   4 s_____

B Copy these verbs. Next to each one write the family word you used in section **A**.

1 close   2 ride   3 smile   4 shake

C Write a sentence describing what happens to words ending in **e** when **ing** is added.

Words ending in **'magic' e** drop the **e** when **ing** is added.

blaze   blaz**ing**   hide   hid**ing**

A Copy and complete each of these word sums.

1 live + ing =   2 save + ing =   3 care + ing =

4 tame + ing =   5 shame + ing =   6 shine + ing =

7 strive + ing =   8 slope + ing =   9 smile + ing =

B Make up six more similar word sums yourself.

Extension

Words ending in **'magic' e** <u>keep</u> the **e** when a suffix that begins with a consonant is added.

hop**e** + **f**ul = hopeful   tun**e** + **l**ess = tuneless

Words ending in **'magic' e** <u>drop</u> the **e** when a suffix that begins with a vowel is added.

cur**e** + **a**ble = curable   jok**e** + **e**r = joker

Remember, **a e i o u** are the vowel letters; the rest are **consonants**.

A Write as many words as you can by combining the root words with the suffixes from the vowel suffix box and the consonant suffix box.

Root words					
use recognise combine rehearse scribble response believe improve excite like hope sense age large					

Vowel suffixes	Consonant suffixes
able ing ed er est ible al ism	ly ful ment less

B List other root words ending in **e** that use each of the suffixes in the two suffix boxes.

tricky words

Key Words

sacrifice
criticise
muscle
prejudice
privilege
language
sincerely
especially
accident
edge
enforce

competition
explanation
profession
pronunciation
persuade
frequently
immediate
equipment
development

Focus

A Copy the list of key words neatly into your book.

B Each of the eight words hidden in the puzzle box is in the key words list and has a **soft c** or a **soft g**. As you find them, tick them off on your list.

d	r	s	e	w	d	g	h	j
b	l	a	n	g	u	a	g	e
v	c	c	m	u	s	c	l	e
c	r	i	t	i	c	i	s	e
p	r	i	v	i	l	e	g	e
e	n	f	o	r	c	e	t	d
z	s	i	d	f	g	h	g	g
a	c	c	i	d	e	n	t	e
p	r	e	j	u	d	i	c	e

Words can be tricky to spell when they
have double letters, such as:

accommodate emba**rr**ass po**ss**e**ss**ion

Each of these words is misspelt because one
of its letters should have been doubled.
Use a dictionary to help you spell them
correctly in your book.

1 comunicate   2 corespond   3 haras   4 recomend

5 guarante   6 ocupy   7 ocur   8 programe

9 profesion   10 agressive   11 atached   12 apreciate

Extension

A Here are some more frequently misspelt words.
Write them correctly, using a dictionary to help
where necessary.

    1 awkword   2 interfear   3 systom

    4 determrined   5 fourty   6 twelth

    7 varity   8 neccessary   9 especally

    10 frequantly   11 immediatley   12 reconise

B Use three of them in sentences to indicate
their meanings.

using a thesaurus

Aa

ability noun
1 *You have the ability to do very well at school.*
  • capability
  • intelligence
2 *He's a young footballer with a lot of ability.*
  • talent
  • skill
  • flair

about adverb
  There are about thirty children in our class.
  • roughly
  • approximately

accept verb
  The children stepped forward to accept their prizes.
  • to take
  • to receive
  opposite reject

accident noun
1 *There was an accident on the main road.*
  • a crash
  • a smash
  • a collision
  • a pile-up
  • a bump
    A pile-up is a bad accident with a lot of cars:
    There was a huge pile-up on the motorway.

A bump is an accident that is not very bad:
We had a bit of a bump on the way to the supermarket.
2 *I'm sorry, it was an accident*
  • a mistake

accidentally adverb
  I accidentally knocked the lamp over.
  • unintentionally
  • inadvertently
  opposite deliberately

accurate adjective
  She gave the police an accurate description of the thief.
  • exact
  • precise
  • correct
  opposite inaccurate

achieve verb
  You have achieved a lot this term.
  • to do
  • to accomplish

achievement noun
  Winning a gold medal is a great achievement
  • an accomplishment
  • a feat
  • a success

act verb
1 *We must act quickly to save these animals.*
  • to do something
  • to take action
2 *I would love to act on the stage.*
  • to perform
  • to appear

a b c d e f g h i j k l m n o p q r s t u v w x y z

l

Key Words

thesaurus
synonym
similar
antonym
opposite

noun
verb
adjective
adverb

example
sample

Focus

A thesaurus is used if we want to find similar or better words to improve our writing.

A Look at the thesaurus page above to find a synonym for these words.

1 about   2 to act   3 to accept
4 achievement   5 accurate

B Copy these sentences using another word to replace the underlined ones.

1 I <u>accidentally</u> bumped into the old lady.
2 There are <u>about</u> 300 children in our school.
3 It would be great if I can <u>act</u> in the school play.
4 My teacher thinks I have the <u>ability</u> to get into the school team.

Copy these words and next to each write an antonym (opposite).
The page opposite will help with some answers but you'll need to look in a thesaurus to find the others.

1 accurate   2 accept

3 accidentally   4 happiness

5 scarce   6 abundant

7 wide   8 excited

9 cool   10 interesting

Use a thesaurus to help you to improve these sentences. Write them in your book.

1 My friend said that my new clothes were <u>nice</u>.

2 Dad has <u>got</u> a new car.

3 I <u>like</u> ice cream.

4 We saw a <u>big</u> crash on the main road.

5 It tasted <u>bad</u>.

6 The athletes came on to the stage to <u>get</u> their medals.

7 That man <u>pinched</u> his mobile phone.

8 What a <u>terrible</u> smell!

> Think particularly about the underlined words.

Check-up 2

Focus

What are these?
Some letters are shown to give you a clue. Write the words in your book.

1 n_____

2 p_____

3 p_____

4 s_____

5 r_____

6 l_____

7 e_____

8 p_____

9 sh_____

10 kn_____

11 s_____

12 w_____

13 d_____

14 ch_____

15 b_____

16 a_____

Extra

A Write the contractions for these words in your book.

1 have not   2 she is   3 could not   4 do not   5 I will

B Complete these words with **oll**, **oal** or **ole**.

1 f_____ (a young horse)   2 r_____ (small type of bread)

3 p_____ (you raise a flag with this)   4 sh_____ (large group of fish)

C Write a homophone for each of these words.

1 bridal   2 mourning   3 guest   4 aloud   5 draft

D Write these words with the **ous** or **ious** suffix added.

1 victor   2 labour   3 vigour   4 glamour   5 fury

E Add **ly** to make adverbs of these words.

1 musical   2 official   3 essential   4 partial   5 clinical

F Write the plural form of these words.

1 wolf   2 shelf   3 leaf   4 chief   5 knife   6 difficulty
7 valley   8 activity   9 injury   10 boy

G Write a homophone for each of these words.

1 way   2 ate   3 vain   4 rain   5 slay

H Copy and complete each of these word sums.

1 save + ing =   2 care + ful =
3 excite + ment =   4 large + est =

I Write each of these misspelt words correctly.

1 recomend   2 guarante   3 ocupy   4 profesion   5 atached

A Something is missing from these adjectives.
Write them correctly in your book.

  1 oven ready   2 quick thinking   3 over rated   4 accident prone

B Add **all** or **al** to make these words.

  1 __together   2 __ready   3 sm__   4 __though   5 __ways

C Use each of these near homophones in a sentence that shows its meaning.

  1 desert   dessert   2 dissent   descent

D Write the **ious** family word for these words.

  1 space   2 infection   3 caution   4 nutrition   5 ambition

E Finish these words, adding either **cial** or **tial**.

  1 spe_____   2 confiden_____   3 spa_____

  4 artifi_____   5 essen_____

F Write each of these misspelt words correctly.

  1 definately   2 intresting   3 immediatley   4 neccessary   5 fourty